Our Kindness Feeds Others

The END HUNGER Book

**by Noelani Musicaro
& Robert Alan Silverstein
*The Kindness Team***

Proceeds from the sale of this book benefit
The Kindness Team,
a non-profit project of We, The World,
dedicated to raising awareness
about the healing and transformative power of kindness,
particularly in the effort to end hunger in America.

TheKindnessTeam.org

ISBN-13: 978-1492396468
ISBN-10: 149239646X

*"Our kindness feeds others...
We can end hunger through kindness!"
-- Noelani Musicaro*

Introduction

Having enough to eat is our fundamental birthright. No one should go hungry. There is enough for everyone. We should be making sure that everyone eats well, no matter who they are. In 2006, the United States changed its definitions and eliminated references to hunger. Instead, the government now uses the phrase "food insecurity" to describe various categories of hunger. Food insecurity means that the food intake of household members is reduced and normal eating patterns disrupted, not knowing where to find the next meal, unable to consistently access nutritious and adequate amounts of food, because the household lacks money and other resources for food. This means that people go hungry.

The face of hunger has changed. In the United States, hunger is a reality, a different reality from what we might think or are told. It is a reality that hunger is not confined to small pockets of society or neighborhoods. These are often hard-working adults (working hungry), children and seniors who simply cannot make ends meet and are forced to go without food for several meals or days. Hungry adults miss more work and consume more health care than those who don't go hungry. Families who once managed can no longer because something happened such as job loss or sickness. Those experiencing hunger are more likely to suffer from anxiety, depression, behavior problems, and other illnesses; this is a major crisis. Unfortunately, food insecurity is an obstacle that threatens establishing and maintaining the critical foundation that has implications on a child's physical and mental health.

After the onset of the financial and economic crisis that erupted in 2008, a dramatic increase in hunger occurred and remains high in the United States. This high level of hunger not only continues, but it is rising. *Hunger is increasing in the United States at an alarming rate. Obesity is everywhere, yet, we are a starving nation.* WIC (Woman Infants Children) is a federal food and nutrition service program to safeguard the health of those with low-income who are at nutritional risk. 50% of babies born in America are participating in WIC. The total cost of hunger to American society is said to be about $90 billion a year. In contrast, it would only cost about $10 billion to $12 billion a year to virtually end hunger in our nation. *In the United States, hunger is not caused by a scarcity of food, but rather the continued prevalence of poverty.*

In many ways, America is the land of plenty. The USDA recently found that about 96 billion pounds of food available for human consumption in the United States were thrown away by retailers, restaurants, farmers and households over the course of one year. This is a forgotten political issue. Poverty and hunger are never discussed. It is silent, an 'unpopular' topic, keeping the poor invisible and out of the dialog.

We can change it - truth against power. Time to stand up and shout.

Poverty in the United States

The official poverty measure is published by the United States Census Bureau shows that: In 2010, 46.9 million people were in poverty, up from 37.3 million in 2007 - the fourth consecutive annual increase in the number of people in poverty. This is the largest number in the 52 years for which poverty rates have been published. **20.5 million** American family's cash income is less than half of the poverty line, or about $10,000 a year for a family of four. 77% of Americans live paycheck to paycheck. Most poverty comes from wages not enough to pay for the basics. Until we agree that, as a country, people have a right to earn a living wage, this is not acceptable and is an unbearable situation. We must come together to confront hunger and poverty in the United States.

A study from Indiana University says the number of Americans living below the poverty line surged by 27% since the beginning of the 2006 recession, driving 10 million more people into poverty. "Poverty in American is widespread. People living in poverty is increasing and expected to increase further, despite the 'recovery'", concludes the study.

Hunger and poverty are tragedies, far more prevalent in America than ever imagined.

Our kindness feeds others. Let's start a kindness revolution. Shift the paradigm.

You matter. Your choices matter. You are powerful. Without you, nothing changes.

"We will forever be known by the tracks we leave behind." – Dakota proverb

With love and gratitude,
Noelani

"We are an advanced third world country living a myth."
- Ralph Nader

"One of the greatest feelings in the world is knowing that
we as individuals can make a difference.
Ending hunger in America is a goal that is
literally within our grasp."
– Jeff Bridges

Table of Contents

"...when Americans learn the facts and understand
how their involvement can make a difference,
banishing childhood hunger will be a national,
local and personal priority."
-- Martin Sheen

Hunger Is a Big Problem

We all know what it's like to be hungry sometimes when we're late for a meal. But some kids and their families are hungry almost all the time because they don't have enough food to eat or safe water to drink.

Hunger is a big problem around the world. Over 850 million people go hungry -- They eat less than the minimum amount of calories they need to be healthy. Even in America, 50 million people go hungry too often, including 1 out of 5 children.

Each year more than a million people die from hunger and hunger-related diseases. Most of them are kids!

Hunger has always been a problem in our world. In the past, one of the reasons was that there just wasn't enough food available for everyone to eat. But in today's world there is plenty of food to go around, and yet people are still starving. This just shouldn't be. The good news is that together We Can end world hunger!

"Many people think that hunger is unavoidable
in any society... That is not true...
America, which leads the world in so many ways,
can end childhood hunger within its borders."
-- Pierce Brosnan

All the World's Leaders Agreed to End World Hunger

Most people would agree that no one should have to starve to death in a world where there is more than enough food for everyone to eat.

In fact, when the leaders of the world met at the United Nations at the Millennium Summit in the year 2000, they agreed to commit themselves to accomplish eight 'Millennium Development Goals' by the year 2015. The first of those goals is to reduce in half the number of people in extreme poverty without the food they need to live healthy lives.

Many of the diverse movements for change that make up the vast 'movement for a better world' have embraced the Millennium Development Goals as tangible achievements to strive towards, and a specific promise and agenda we can insist that our leaders honor.

Is our nation living up to their promise of working to eliminate hunger? United for a better world, we can convince our leaders that we must honor that promise to end world hunger!

*"If you want to eliminate hunger,
everybody has to be involved."
-- Bono*

Ways To End Hunger

There are three different avenues that people, organizations and governments are pursuing to help to end world hunger.

Since as many as 40,000 people die every day from hunger, the first and most urgent way to help, is to provide food for those who are hungry. There are many local, national and international organizations that help deliver life-saving food supplies around the world to those who suffer from hunger because of poverty, disasters or war. In the US an extensive system of **food banks** allows excess food, collected from supermarkets and individuals, to be given to people in need. Many rely on **soup kitchens** in community buildings and places of worship for a warm meal. Government programs like **food stamps** and **school breakfast and lunch programs** help prevent many families from going without meals.

The next step is to help people and their communities to find sustainable ways to feed themselves, through education and improving agricultural practices. The long-term solution to the problem of hunger is to find the reasons why people are going hungry, and to address those root causes. As the BetterWorld Movement strives to create a more peaceful, just and sustainable world, we are working towards creating a world without hunger.

Policies To End Hunger

In the 1960s and 1970s, hunger was nearly wiped out in America thanks to a bipartisan plan by the federal government to create and expand nutrition programs for children and the elderly. But over the last few years, the government's support of these programs has decreased, and the number of Americans who go hungry has skyrocketed.

Many hunger organizations work to directly get food to those who are hungry through food banks, soup kitchens, and services like Meals On Wheels, but organizations also work hard to try to convince government officials to once again strengthen support for the successful programs that can help eliminate hunger.

The programs that organizations want the government to strengthen include: **Food Stamps,** which help more than 25 million people with low incomes get the food for their families they need to survive; The **School Breakfast and School Lunch** programs which provide free and reduced-price meals to over 22 million school children; and the Special Supplemental Nutrition Program for Women, Infants, and Children, better known as **WIC**, which provides nutritious food, nutrition counseling, and health care referrals to 8 million low-income women, infants and children.

"There can be no lasting peace, no security,
nor can we as human beings begin to touch our full
potential, as long as hunger overwhelms the
human spirit around this planet."
-- Dennis Weaver

Portrait of a BetterWorld Hero

John van Hengel set out to change his life and ended up changing the world. After a divorce and serious injury, he relocated to Arizona and got involved in several charities. While volunteering at a soup kitchen, a woman told him that she often got the food to feed her children by going through grocery store garbage cans. She told him that the food was perfectly good and that, just as there is a bank to store money, there should be a place to store excess food until people needed it.

With this idea as his inspiration, John van Hengel contacted local groceries and bakeries and in 1967 he set up the St. Mary's Foodbank in Phoenix, Arizona -- the first food bank.

In 1976 John van Hengel started America's Second Harvest - a national food bank network that has grown to include more than 200 food banks that donate food to 50,000 agencies which provide food for 23 million Americans.

"It's amazing how many people are being fed because of this crazy little thing we started. We're feeding millions and it is not costing anyone anything."
-- John van Hengel

"There are genuinely sufficient resources in the world
to ensure that no one, nowhere,
at no time, should go hungry."
– Edward Asner

End Hunger Days

World Food Day – October 16

World Food Day is an important opportunity to come together to raise awareness about the urgent problem of world hunger and inspire year-round activities to ensure food security for all. Local, national and global events are organized each year. In the United States, observances are coordinated by The United States National Committee for World Food Day -- a coalition of 450 non-profit organizations. **We** can help publicize existing events and activities, as well as create new local fairs, festivals and house parties to spread the message that **We Can End Hunger**!

http://BetterWorldCalendar.org/EndHungerDay.htm

Hunger Action Month

Feeding America promotes the month of September as Hunger Awareness Month and helps coordinate events and activities all month-long to raise awareness about the serious issue of hunger in America and to inspire people to get involved in helping in their communities.   In addition to volunteering during the month of September and all year long at a local food bank or soup kitchen, they suggest that you wear orange to show your support. You can also change your Facebook, Twitter and other social media profiles to orange to inspire others to get involved.

http://feedingamerica.org/get-involved/hunger-action-month.aspx
http://facebook.com/FeedingAmerica

"In a nutshell, this United Nations non-profit organization
[World Food Programme] feeds millions of starving
children at schools in third world countries
as an incentive for them to attend school,
which in turn might better their futures."
-- Sheryl Crow

The United Nations

Ending hunger is one of the United Nations' most important goals. There are two United Nations agencies specifically devoted to addressing the important issue of **food security** -- ensuring that all people have access all of the time to the food that they need to lead healthy lives.

Since its founding in 1945, **FAO, the Food and Agriculture Organization** of the United Nations, has been helping to lead international efforts to end world hunger. The agency provides information and expertise to developing countries, helping to improve agriculture, fisheries and forestry practices to increase the available food supply and provide better nutrition. FAO also provides a forum where representatives of all nations can debate international policies and negotiate international agreements to help build a world without hunger.

www.FAO.org

The World Food Programme (WFP) is the United Nations agency that works to meet emergency needs for food around the world in times of disasters, for refugees and in the ongoing battle to feed the world's poor who have no access to food. It also promotes policies that support economic and social development that will benefit the world's poor and hungry.

www.WFP.org

"Because the suffering of any human being diminishes all
of us, it's our responsibility to try to ease that suffering.
It is not a matter of titles,
but of responsibilities."
-- Khaled

14

International Alliance To End Hunger

The UN's World Food Summit Plan of Action in 1996 and the Millennium Development Goals set the stage for a global effort to end hunger. In 2002, the International Alliance to End Hunger was formed to coordinate efforts between UN and international food agencies with national programs around the world.

The FAO Ambassadors Programme was created to enlist global personalities to help attract public and media attention to the work of the International Alliance. Following is an excerpt from the FAO Pledge.

"...Humankind has the power to effect change: to end hunger, to fight poverty and disease, and to banish illiteracy. We cannot tolerate hunger and malnutrition. We have the techniques and the resources to eliminate them. What is lacking is human solidarity and political will. For this reason, we, the FAO Ambassadors:

pledge to inspire people everywhere to work together in an International Alliance against Hunger;

call upon all people to help the least privileged people of the world finally to break out of the vicious circle of chronic hunger, poverty and under-nourishment, and make a world where everyone has reliable access to safe and nutritious food;

commit ourselves to use our talents and unique opportunities to help increase awareness and raise funds for the fight against hunger.

For us, the drive to defeat hunger is a question of personal responsibility. We want to be part of a generation that has achieved this goal. **Please join hands with us in the International Alliance Against Hunger.**

www.iaahp.net

"Peace can only last where human rights are respected,
where the people are fed, and where individuals
and nations are free."
-- The Dalai Lama

Organizations Helping
to End Hunger

There are many little things that all of us can do to help end hunger. But if ending hunger is your passion for a better world, there are many organizations that you can help support financially, or become involved with. Following are just a few.

Alliance to End Hunger includes businesses, civil rights groups, labor unions, religious bodies and universities devoted to shifting U.S. public opinion, policy and institutions to end hunger. **Alliance to End Hunger** | 425 3rd Street SW, Suite 1200, Washington, DC 20024 | **Tel: 202-639-9400** | **Web: www.alliancetoendhunger.org**

AmpleHarvest.org helps connect more than 40 million Americans with excess food in their gardens to local food pantries that supply food to the hungry in their communities. **Ample Harvest | info@AmpleHarvest.org | ampleharvest.org**

Blessings in a Backpack provides backpacks full of food to hungry schoolchildren every Friday to ensure impoverished elementary school children are fed on the weekends. They currently feed over 50,000 children in 376 schools across 39 U.S. states and three countries. **Blessings in a Backpack | 4121 Shelbyville Rd Louisville, KY 40207 | 1-800-872 – 4366 | www.blessingsinabackpack.org**

"...just a fraction of what is extended so obscenely on
defense budgets would make a real difference in enabling
God's children to fill their stomachs,
be educated, and be given the chance to
lead fulfilled and happy lives."
-- Desmond Tutu

Bread for the World is a Christian movement that includes 2,500 churches that lobby U.S. decision makers on legislation dealing with hunger in America and around the world. **Bread for the World | 425 3rd Street SW, Suite 1200 | Washington, DC 20024 | (800-82-BREAD) | www.Bread.org**

End Hunger Network was started by actor Jeff Bridges to rally the entertainment industry to support media events and programs which encourage the public to get involved in helping to end childhood hunger. **End Hunger Network | 3819 Hunt Manor Drive | Fairfax VA 22033 | (703) 860-1273 | www.EndHunger.com**

Feed The Children is a Christian relief organization that delivers food, clothing and medicine to families that are hungry due to poverty, war, famine and natural disasters. **Feed The Children | PO Box 36 | Oklahoma City, OK 73101-0036 | (800) 627-4556 | www.feedthechildren.org**

Feeding America is the nation's largest network of food banks and food rescue organizations serving every county in the United States. **Feeding America| 35 E. Wacker Dr., #2000 | Chicago, IL 60601 | (800) 771-2303 | (312) 263-2303 | www.feedingamerica.org**

FoodCorps places motivated leaders in communities with limited resources for a year of public service to teach kids about healthy food, build school gardens and bring high-quality food into public cafeterias. **FoodCorps, Inc. | 281 Park Avenue South | New York, NY 10010 | info@foodcorps.org | foodcorps.org**

19

"I can't think of any issue that is more important
than working to see that no schoolchild
in this world goes hungry."
-- Drew Barrymore

Food Policy Action lobbies to promote policies that support affordable, safe food and healthy diets to reduce hunger at home and abroad. **Food Policy Action | 1436 U St. N.W. Suite 200, Washington, DC 20009 | foodpolicyaction.org**

Making Change, formerly Food For All, works with over 8000 supermarkets in the Point-of-Purchase program, where customers can add a small donation to hunger organizations to their shopping bill at the checkout counter. **Making Change | 3101 Park Center Drive, Suite 108 | Alexandria, VA 22302 | (888) 960-6435 | www. makingchange.org**

Oxfam America provides emergency hunger relief as well as focusing on campaigns to address changes in global policies and practices that cause hunger to continue in our world. **Oxfam America | 226 Causeway St., 5th Floor | Boston, MA 02114-2206 | (800) 77-OXFAM | www.oxfamamerica.org**

World Hunger Year (WHY), started by folk singer Harry Chapin, works with local organizations to promote grassroots solutions to ending hunger and connecting these organizations to funders, media and legislators. WHY sponsors the Hungerthon on TV each year which provides information about hunger and poverty to 6 million viewers. An annual Awards Dinner also honors grassroots organizations with publicity and a cash grant. **World Hunger Year | 505 Eighth Ave, Suite 2100 | New York, NY 10018 | (212) 629-8850 | www.worldhungeryear.org**

"*Every gun that is made, every warship launched,
every rocket fired signifies, in the final sense,
a theft from those who hunger and are not fed,
those who are cold and are not clothed.*"
-- Dwight D. Eisenhower

Valuable Resources

LOCATE A LOCAL HUNGER ORGANIZATION SO YOU CAN VOLUNTEER:
http://endhunger.com/volunteer.html

LOCATE A LOCAL FOOD BANK:
http://feedamerica.org/foodbank-results.aspx

NEED HELP FINDING FOOD?
National Hunger Hotline
1-866-3-HUNGRY
http://whyhunger.org/findfood

GET INSPIRED!
BetterWorldQuotes.com/endhunger-quotes.htm

Feeding Minds Fighting Hunger: A World Without Hunger is a free curriculum available on the internet in a dozen different languages that strives to inspire and empower young people and their teachers to "actively participate in creating a world free from hunger." **www.feedingminds.org**

Blueprint to End Hunger is another free resource to help educate and inspire action.

www.jeffbridges.com/blueprinttoendhunger.pdf

Eat Healthy – Feed The World

Did you know that when you eat a healthier diet, consider more vegetarian options, and don't waste food, you're helping end world hunger! Why a vegetarian diet? It takes 15 to 20 pounds of grains to produce 1 pound of meat. The grains and soybeans fed to American livestock each year would feed 1.3 billion starving people.

*"Many things made me become a vegetarian,
among them, the higher food yield
as a solution to world hunger."*
-- John Denver

"A diet higher in whole grains and legumes and lower in beef and other meat is not just healthier for ourselves but also contributes to changing the world system that feeds some people and leaves others hungry."
-- Dr. Walden Bello

"How unthinkable that, in a country of such bursting plenty, so many people are facing ongoing hunger and poverty. If we are truly each other's keepers, let's support school lunches, food stamps, neighborhood garden projects, and so many other wonderful programs working to put an end to this cruel and needless blight once and for all."
-- Bonnie Raitt

You Can Help End Hunger

1. Pledge to volunteer 5 hours a month in a local soup kitchen or food pantry and donate food items to your local food pantry each month.

2. Donate money to The Kindness Team or a local, national or international nonprofit organization working to end hunger in America and around the world.

3. Make thehungersite.com your homepage and click on it every day – sponsors pay for food for the hungry with every click.

4. Get the word out – talk to your friends and family about the problem of poverty and hunger and help get them involved.

5. Contact your leaders and let them know that ending hunger is a big priority. Visit the One Campaign's website and sign the ONE CAMPAIGN Declaration urging our leaders to honor the Millennium Development Goals, and wear the white band to show others your support. (**www.onecampaign.org**)

6. Skip a meal for hunger and donate the cost of the meal to hunger organizations. Host a Hunger Banquet and invite others to join you. **www.oxfamamerica.org**

Wear the White Band and
Sign the One Declaration

"WE BELIEVE that in the best American tradition of helping others help themselves, now is the time to join with other countries in a historic pact for compassion and justice to help the poorest people of the world overcome AIDS and extreme poverty. WE RECOGNIZE that a pact including such measures as fair trade, debt relief, fighting corruption and directing additional resources for basic needs – education, health, clean water, food, and care for orphans – would transform the futures and hopes of an entire generation in the poorest countries, at a cost equal to just one percent more of the US budget. WE COMMIT ourselves - one person, one voice, one vote at a time - to make a better, safer world for all."

www.OneCampaign.org

"There is enough for everybody's need,
but not for everybody's greed."
-- Mohandas K. Gandhi

29

"I want a different world. One where I don't wake up
thinking I'm so lucky to be able to feed my daughter, and
able to give people a clean drink of water.
I don't want images of starving babies
at the breast in my mind. I want that to change.
And if I want that, I had better do something about it."
-- Emma Thompson

THE KINDNESS TEAM
Our Kindness Feeds Others
Changing the World, One Kind Heart At a Time
TheKindnessTeam.org

THE KINDNESS TEAM is dedicated to raising awareness about the healing and transformative power of kindness, particularly in the effort to end hunger in America. The Kindness Team is the birthchild of Noelani Musicaro and Robert Alan Silverstein, and includes a network of kind people whose mission is to spread the idea of kindness in the world, changing the paradigm, changing the world - one kind heart at a time. Kindness is everything.

THE KINDNESS TEAM is a **NON-PROFIT** project of **We, The World** (WE.Net). Funds are used to create educational materials and videos to inspire and empower action to end hunger and promote kindness.

THE KINDNESS TEAM consists of:

Noelani Musicaro is CEO, Creative Director and Founder/Owner, of www.FiglieDiFortuna.com and www.TheKindnessConversations.com. Noelani is a visionary/social entrepreneur, artist, author, healing facilitator, novice musician, former candidate for Lt. Governor of New Jersey (Independent, 2009), former host of Cablevision's "Artertainment", and volunteer (Red Cross Disaster Team, Grace Hospice). She is an intrepid traveler, is curious and wondrous, and a warrior of truth and light.

Robert Alan Silverstein is a utopian author, artist, songwriter, filmmaker, webmaster and social change activist. Since he created The People for Peace Project in 1995, hundreds of thousands of activists and students have been inspired by his educational resources that integrate his illustrations of more than 1,000 Better World Heroes for a more peaceful, just and sustainable world. Robert has served as an NGO Representative to the United Nations, as the managing director of a small philanthropic grant-making foundation, and as the coordinator of several global campaigns for a better world.

Adjunct: Peter Felperin
AND YOU!

Please contact us! We love people and would love to hear from you!
MyKindnessFeedsOthers@gmail.com

Please donate to help raise and spread awareness about the healing and transformative power of kindness, particularly in the effort to end hunger in America. Go to www.TheKindnessTeam.org.

Thank you!!

The Kindness Team Books

*Proceeds benefit our non-profit work
to promote kindness and end hunger in America*

 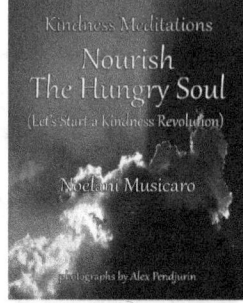 

**For a complete catalog visit our website:
The Kindness Team.org**

*Coming soon:
The Kindness Conversations
– A Series of Interviews About Kindness*

www.ingramcontent.com/pod-product-compliance
Lightning Source LLC
Chambersburg PA
CBHW070845290526
45795CB00002B/992